I0816923

WEIRD WORLD

WEIRD ANIMALS

BY EMMA KAISER

Core Library

An Imprint of Abdo Publishing
abdobooks.com

Cover image: The male magnificent frigate bird inflates its red throat pouch to attract mates.

abdobooks.com

Published by Abdo Publishing, a division of ABDO, PO Box 398166, Minneapolis, Minnesota 55439.

Printed in the United States of America, North Mankato, Minnesota.
102025
012026

Cover Photo: Shutterstock Images
Interior Photos: Paul Starosta/Stone/Getty Images, 4–5; Karl H. Switak/Science Source, 6; Shutterstock Images, 8, 23, 39; Dave Watts/Science Source, 10–11; Marie Read/Science Source, 13; Joerg Sarbach/AP Images, 15; Don Mammoser/Shutterstock Images, 18–19; Angela N. Perryman/Shutterstock Images, 20; William Cushman/Shutterstock Images, 22, 45; Alfredo Maiquez/Shutterstock Images, 26–27, 43; Bence Mate/NaturePL/Science Source, 28–29; Cede Prudente/NHPA/Photoshot/Science Source, 31; Jojo Dexter/Shutterstock Images, 33; John A. Anderson/Shutterstock Images, 34–35; Mayumi K. Photography/Shutterstock Images, 36; Peter David/Science Source, 38

Editor: Riley Madsen
Series Designer: Marley Richmond

Library of Congress Control Number: 2025939170

Publisher's Cataloging-in-Publication Data

Names: Kaiser, Emma, author.
Title: Weird animals / by Emma Kaiser
Description: Minneapolis, Minnesota: Abdo Publishing, 2026 | Series: Weird world | Includes online resources and index.
Identifiers: ISBN 9781098298463 (lib. bdg.) | ISBN 9798384932260 (ebook)
Subjects: LCSH: Oddities--Juvenile literature. | Animals--Juvenile literature. | Animal behavior--Juvenile literature. | Nature--Juvenile literature. | Curiosities and wonders--Juvenile literature.
Classification: DDC 591.4--dc23

CONTENTS

ANIMAL ADAPTATIONS

In the tropical forests of western Africa, a Cameroonian hunter stalks along a riverbank. He keeps his eyes on the water. He is hunting for a creature that will make a delicious meal. But this creature is not easy to catch. The water is murky, but the hunter sees something move beneath its surface. He uses a long spear to strike the water. When he pulls back the spear, he sees he was successful. On the spear's tip is a small frog. But this frog is unique. It has a hairy fringe growing along its sides. The hunter has to be

Besides Cameroon, hairy frogs also live in countries such as Nigeria, Equatorial Guinea, the Democratic Republic of the Congo, and Gabon.

Female hairy frogs and males outside of the mating season typically do not have fringes.

careful when handling the frog. At the end of its feet are sharp, curved claws that extend from the toes. The hunter knows from experience that these claws can easily cut and draw blood.

This frog is known as the hairy frog. It's also called the wolverine frog or the horror frog. This amphibian gets its name from its unique appearance. During mating season, the males grow a thick fringe along their sides. Though the bristles look like hair, they're actually more like scales. The fringe works as a temporary organ. Scientists believe the blood vessels in this fringe help the frog breathe better, especially when underwater. A male hairy frog can stay underwater for up to several days while guarding its mate's eggs.

This frog's claws are actually thorn-shaped bones inside its toes. When the hairy frog flexes its foot muscles, the bones pivot, slicing through the frog's skin to form claws. Eventually, the bones move back into place and the frog's skin heals. The claws remain covered until the frog is ready to use them again. Scientists believe the frog extends its claws against predators or hunters when it feels threatened.

AWESOME AMPHIBIANS

Amphibians include frogs, toads, newts, salamanders, and other animals. More than 8,200 amphibian species live on Earth. Amphibians can be found on every continent except Antarctica. They can live in rainforests, rivers and streams, deserts, and mountains. Many amphibians can breathe through their skin. Their skin can also protect them from diseases.

HOW ANIMALS ADAPT

Animals have developed many strange and interesting

CLASSIFICATION OF ANIMALS

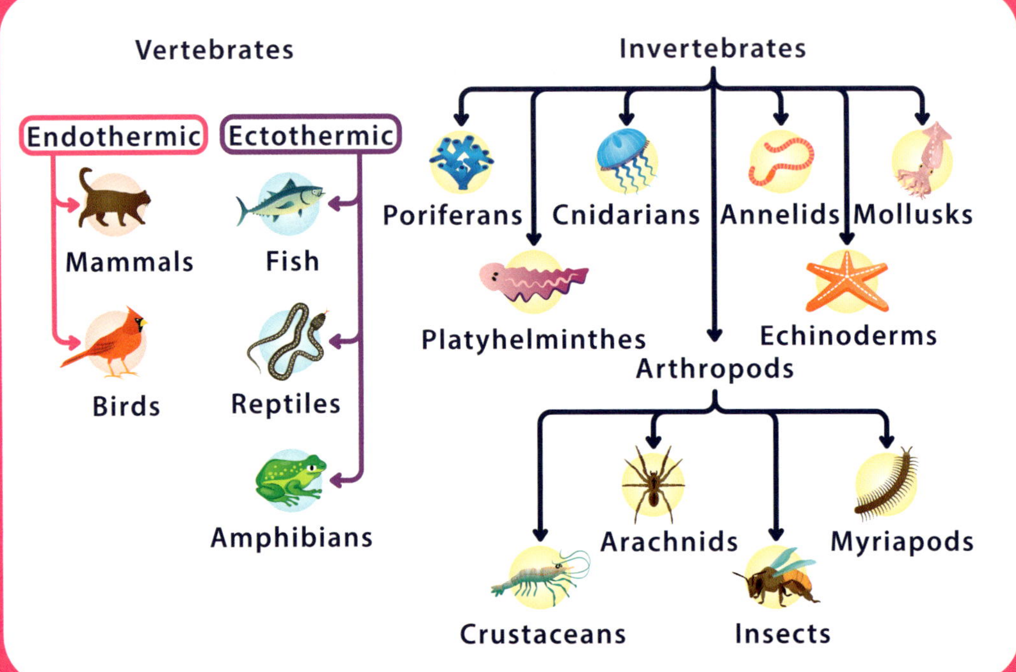

Animals can be classified into different groups according to shared traits and evolutionary relationships. How does this chart of animal classification help you better understand the text?

strategies to help them survive in the wild. Sometimes, these adaptations give them an odd appearance. Some animals develop unique abilities that give them an advantage over other species. These abilities can help animals survive in extreme or harsh habitats. They can help animals hunt, eat, or reproduce.

A process called natural selection helps explain why animals develop weird traits. Natural selection is a process of evolution. It describes how living things change over time. Sometimes animals experience mutations in their genes. These genetic accidents may give animals new traits that could prove harmful or helpful. If a trait hurts an animal, the animal will likely die and not pass on that trait to its offspring. If the trait helps the animal survive, the animal is more likely to pass that trait to its offspring. That trait may help the next generation survive too. The weirdest animals in the world have some very weird traits.

THE ASP CATERPILLAR

The asp caterpillar is another creature known for its strange, hairy appearance. This caterpillar is covered in long, white hairs. However, these strands contain sharp, poisonous spines. If they pierce the skin, they can cause blisters, nausea, headaches, and breathing problems. This poison protects the caterpillar from predators, giving it a better chance to grow into its adult form.

CHAPTER TWO

MYSTIFYING MAMMALS

Mammals are a class of animals. Mammals are vertebrates that give birth to live young and produce milk to feed them. Mammals have hair. And almost all mammals are endothermic, which means they can control their own body temperature. But some mammals stand out within their class. These mammals are exceptions to the rules.

The platypus is one such mammal. At first glance, the platypus looks as if it has the features of several different animals. It lives in rivers

The platypus is mostly nocturnal, which means that it hunts at night and sleeps during the day.

and lakes in Australia. When British scientists first studied the body of a platypus, they thought it was a prank. They thought it was made of body parts from different animals sewn together. The platypus has a flat body and waterproof fur. It has strong front legs and webbed feet for paddling. It also has a large bill similar to a duck. These features make it well adapted for water. Males have spurs on their back legs that can release venom. This venom is strong enough to kill small animals. But scientists have found substances within platypus venom that could actually be helpful to humans. These substances could be used to treat diabetes.

Although the platypus is classified as a mammal, it does not give birth to live young. It lays eggs. The female lays up to three eggs at a time in a burrow and curls around them to keep them warm. After the eggs hatch, the female platypus nurses the newborn

The platypus's natural prey includes insects, worms, and shellfish.

platypuses, or puggles, for several months. However, the platypus is also one of the few mammals that doesn't produce milk through nipples. Instead, it releases milk through its skin. The process is similar to how other mammals produce sweat. The puggle then laps up the milk off its mother's belly.

ECHIDNA

One other mammal lays eggs and nurses its young like the platypus. It's called the echidna. It is also known as a spiny anteater. This animal is found in Australia, Tasmania, and New Guinea. It's covered in spines that are actually very tough hairs. Female echidnas lay one egg at a time. The egg is kept inside the mother's pouch for ten days before it hatches.

THE NAKED MOLE RAT

The naked mole rat is another exceptional mammal. This rodent has pink, wrinkly skin that's almost transparent. Although the naked mole rat has less hair than many other mammals, it is not completely hairless. It has whiskers on its face, which it uses to feel. It relies

A quarter of the muscle mass of the naked mole rat is found in its powerful jaws.

on its whiskers because it is almost entirely blind. It also has hairs between its toes. These hairs help it sweep away dirt when digging underground tunnels.

Unlike most other mammals, the naked mole rat does not keep a steady body temperature. Its temperature changes based on the temperature of its environment. However, it is dangerous for the naked mole rat to get too hot or too cold. It lives in large colonies underground and sleeps in piles with other naked mole rats to stay warm.

Naked mole rats build elaborate burrows with many rooms and interconnecting tunnels. These tunnels can be more than two miles (3 km) long and six feet (2 m) underground. The naked mole rat uses its large front teeth to help it dig. It almost never appears above ground. It eats the roots of plants. It gets enough moisture from its food so it doesn't have to drink water. These characteristics all help it live in dry regions of eastern Africa.

HAIRY MOTHS

Mammals are the only animals that grow true hair. But other animals can appear hairy. Many moths seem furry or hairy. This fluff is called setae. These hard bristles are features of many insects. The setae serve different purposes. They can keep moths warm. They can also reduce sounds the moths make as they move. This protects them from predators.

STRAIGHT TO THE SOURCE

George Shaw was an English biologist. He worked at the British Museum in the 1790s. He was one of the first European scientists to describe and classify the platypus. In an article called "The Duck-Billed Platypus," Shaw wrote:

> *Of all the Mammalia yet known it seems the most extraordinary in its [appearance], exhibiting the perfect resemblance of the beak of a Duck [attached to] the head of a quadruped. . . . The body is [flattened] and has some resemblance to that of an Otter in miniature: it is covered with a very thick, soft, and beaver-like fur. . . . The tail is flat, furry like the body. . . . I ought perhaps to acknowledge that I almost doubt the testimony of my own eyes.*

Source: George Shaw. "The Duck-Billed Platypus." *The Naturalist's Miscellany*, vol. 10, no. CXVIII, June 1799, biodiversitylibrary.org. Accessed 28 Mar. 2025.

CONSIDER YOUR AUDIENCE

Adapt this passage for a different audience, such as your friends. Write a blog post conveying this same information for the new audience. How does your post differ from the original text and why?

CHAPTER THREE

BIZARRE BIRDS

Scientists have described more than 10,000 species of birds around the world. They come in different shapes, sizes, and colors. Like other animals, birds evolve traits that help them survive in their environments. Whether they live near water or in deserts, in forests or jungles, in cold or heat, they adapt to survive. But some birds develop especially creative ways to eat, nest, and attract mates.

The magnificent frigate bird is a sea bird that lives in tropical regions such as the Caribbean.

The oldest known magnificent frigate bird lived for almost 20 years, but the average lifespan of the species is not known.

Although the magnificent frigate bird does not dive into water, it does skim the water's surface for prey.

It nests on land but spends most of its time in flight above the water. Most sea birds hunt marine animals and have waterproof feathers. But the magnificent frigate bird is not like most sea birds.

The magnificent frigate bird's feathers are not waterproof. It cannot dive for fish or get its wings wet. If its wings get wet, it cannot fly. The bird has developed different ways to feed. One of its strategies involves chasing down other birds. It grasps them and shakes them until they vomit their food. The magnificent frigate bird then eats what the other birds cough up. This method has earned the magnificent frigate bird the nickname "the pirate bird."

The magnificent frigate bird has a few other special features. While it weighs only about five pounds (2 kg), its wingspan can be up to seven feet (2 m) wide. It has the largest weight-to-wingspan ratio of any bird on Earth. Those wings help it ride air currents

BIG-BRAINED CROWS

Crows are among the most intelligent animals. Their brain-to-body ratio is even greater than that of humans. They are also one of only four animals known to use tools. Humans, chimpanzees, and orangutans are the only other such species. Crows will sharpen sticks into spears or hooks to help them reach insects. They will even place nuts on busy roads. The crows wait for cars to run over the nuts. This cracks open the hard shells so the birds can eat the seed inside.

The male magnificent frigate bird's pouch can grow as large as half the size of its body during the mating season.

for as long as a month at a time. It can even sleep for short periods while flying. The magnificent frigate bird is also known for another unique feature. Males have large red pouches on their necks. They inflate these pouches and clap their beaks together to attract mates.

BIRD BUILDERS

Bowerbirds live in New Guinea and Australia. Female bowerbirds are very picky about choosing a mate. Males work hard to impress females. To attract

Males of the satin bowerbird species prefer to add blue items to their bowers. This may be because the items match the color of parts of their plumage.

a mate, male bowerbirds build eye-catching, creative nests. These structures are called bowers. Bowerbirds build bowers out of sticks and twigs. Then they decorate them with bright-colored objects such as stones, flowers, and insect skeletons. Even items left behind by humans, such as glass, plastic, and cloth, can find their way into a bower.

There are 20 different types of bowerbirds. Males display a variety of colors in their feathers. The dullest-colored bowerbirds build the biggest bowers. The Vogelkop gardener bowerbird is plain compared to other bowerbirds. But it builds bowers that are more than five feet (1.5 m) high.

Bowerbird nests also help their environment. Bowers that include fruit are especially attractive to female bower birds. Male bowerbirds bring in nearby fruit. When the fruit dries up, the male birds throw it out. This helps spread the fruit seeds, keeping the habitat healthy.

WHY AUSTRALIA?

Australia is known for having many weird animals. Most of Australia's native animal species are found only in Australia. This is due to its location. Australia is a continent, but it's also an island. This makes it isolated. Most species cannot migrate long distances or interact with other species the way they can on other continents. Therefore, some adaptations do not spread beyond Australia.

STRAIGHT TO THE SOURCE

Researchers have studied how bowerbirds' brain sizes compare to the brain sizes of other birds. In an article published in the journal *Science*, Dutch biologist Menno Schilthuizen writes:

> *As bird behavior goes, the displays of bowerbirds are among the weirdest. Male bowerbirds have taken up architecture to impress females, building large hutlike structures of twigs, decorated with shiny beetles, shells, and other colorful touches. . . . Bowerbirds have substantially larger brains, compared to their body size, than other birds. It seems that building and appreciating designer follies has led to smarter birds. . . . Even within the bowerbirds, the species that build the more imaginative bowers have larger brains for their size than species that tend to cut corners.*
>
> Source: Menno Schilthuizen. "Bowerbirds, Brainy Birds." *Science*, 10 Apr. 2001, science.org. Accessed 21 Feb. 2025.

BACK IT UP

The author of this passage is using evidence to support a point. Write a paragraph describing the point the author is making. Then write down two or three pieces of evidence the author uses to make the point.

REMARKABLE REPTILES

In general, reptiles are vertebrates that are ectothermic, which means they cannot control their own body temperature internally. They have to find external sources of heat to keep warm. Reptiles mostly consist of snakes, turtles, crocodilians, and lizards. Most reptiles lay eggs and have dry, scaly skin. They may live in water or on land. And some reptiles have developed unique ways of moving around.

The green basilisk is a lizard that lives in the rainforests of Central America. Males have

The green basilisk is also known as the plumed basilisk for the crests on its head.

The green basilisk's long tail helps it remain stable during dashes across the water.

bright green crests on their heads and backs. The green basilisk lives mainly in trees and close to bodies of water. It is also known as the "Jesus Christ Lizard."

This is because of its special talent. This lizard can run on water. In the Christian Bible, Jesus Christ is said to have walked on water.

The green basilisk can run across water at more than seven miles per hour (11 kmh). It does this by spreading out its toes to create more contact between the water and its body. Then it pumps its legs and slaps its feet hard against the water. This movement creates tiny pockets of air that helps keep the lizard above the water's surface. It can run as far as 15 feet (4.6 m) across the water. The green basilisk is also a strong swimmer and can stay underwater for up to ten minutes. These adaptions help it outrun and avoid predators.

KOMODO DRAGON

The Komodo dragon is the largest lizard in the world. It can grow up to 10 feet (3 m) long and weigh more than 350 pounds (159 kg). It is also one of the few venomous lizards. The Komodo dragon has venom glands in its lower jaw. This venom, along with the Komodo dragon's razor-sharp teeth, makes its bite deadly. This helps it take down prey of all sizes, from rodents to water buffalo.

FLYING SNAKES

Most snakes use their flexible spines and

Flying snakes are the only limbless vertebrates that are known to glide.

many muscles to slither along the ground. But one type of snake has figured out how to move through the air. Flying snakes are a type of snake found in South Asia.

They can't fly high in the air the way birds can. But they can glide over long distances.

To do this, flying snakes slither off the edges of high tree branches. As they fall, they flatten their bodies. This helps trap air underneath them, similar to how a parachute works. While in the air, the snakes move back and forth in an S shape. This helps them turn in the air.

Scientists don't know exactly why flying snakes developed this skill. But they think it may help the snakes escape predators. It may also help the snakes hunt prey. Flying snakes eat rodents, frogs, birds,

TIGER BEETLE

Speed can help animals flee predators. But speed can also help predators hunt down their prey. Tiger beetles are the fastest insects on the planet. They can travel at eight feet (2.4 m) per second. They move so fast that they temporarily lose their ability to see. They chase down their prey in short bursts. Tiger beetles prefer to hunt in open spaces such as beaches. There, they chase ants, caterpillars, grasshoppers, and other beetles.

Tiger beetles grip and chew food using their powerful mandibles.

bats, and lizards. Their fangs contain mild venom that also helps them take down prey. But this venom is harmless to humans.

FURTHER EVIDENCE

Chapter Four has information about how the green basilisk gets around. What is the main point of this chapter? What key evidence supports this point? Go to the article about the green basilisk at the website below. Find a quote from the article that supports the chapter's main point.

GREEN CRESTED BASILISK

abdocorelibrary.com/weird-animals

CHAPTER FIVE

STRANGE SEA CREATURES

Because Earth's oceans are so vast, it can be very difficult to study the animals that live there. About 80 percent of the ocean has not been explored by humans. Scientists estimate that more than 90 percent of ocean species have yet to be classified or studied. Much of what lies deep beneath the ocean's surface remains a mystery. But the parts scientists have explored hold some pretty amazing animals.

Sea slugs are a type of mollusk. They look like regular snails or slugs, but they live in salt water.

The ocean is home to a vast diversity of life.

The Pikachu sea slug's scientific name is *Thecacera pacifica*.

Most of the time they live in shallower parts of the sea. More than 1,500 kinds of sea slugs live around the world. They have a wide range of appearances. Different kinds look like flowers, leaves, butterflies, other animals, or even mythical creatures. Some can appear cute, silly, or scary.

One sea slug is known as the Pikachu sea slug because it looks like the famous yellow Pokémon.

Another is called the blue dragon because it looks almost as if it has wings. Others are called sea sheep or sea bunnies for their resemblance to the cute and fluffy land animals. Because sea slugs don't have shells like some other mollusks, they must find other ways to protect themselves. Scientists think that sea slugs developed showy exteriors to ward off predators. These exteriors may be signals to predators that the sea slugs are toxic. The slugs can also take on the colors of their surroundings, which helps them camouflage themselves.

Sea slugs have many abilities. Some sea slugs can absorb the toxins or stingers of other sea creatures. If predators later try to eat them, they'll feel a sting or the effects

JELLYFISH

The jellyfish is one type of sea creature that uses stingers. Jellyfish have no brain and are 98 percent water. But they use their stingers to immobilize their prey. Jellyfish keep their stingers in little compartments on their many tentacles. When touched, the compartment opens and lets out the stinger. The stinger then releases venom.

Many species of anglerfish have enormous mouths full of razor-sharp teeth.

of the toxins. Sea slugs can also regenerate body parts that they have lost. Some sea slugs eat algae that live off photosynthesis. The sea slugs then store up the algae in their bodies. This provides the sea slugs with solar-powered energy.

DEEP-SEA FISH

Life can be tough at the bottom of the ocean. Sunlight cannot reach the deepest parts of the ocean floor, which means there is no light and no plants. It can be very hard to find food. Few animals can survive down there. But deep-sea anglerfish have developed a unique

OCEAN ZONES

Sea creatures live at different ocean depths, from the shallows to the ocean floor. How do these different environments shape the animals that live there?

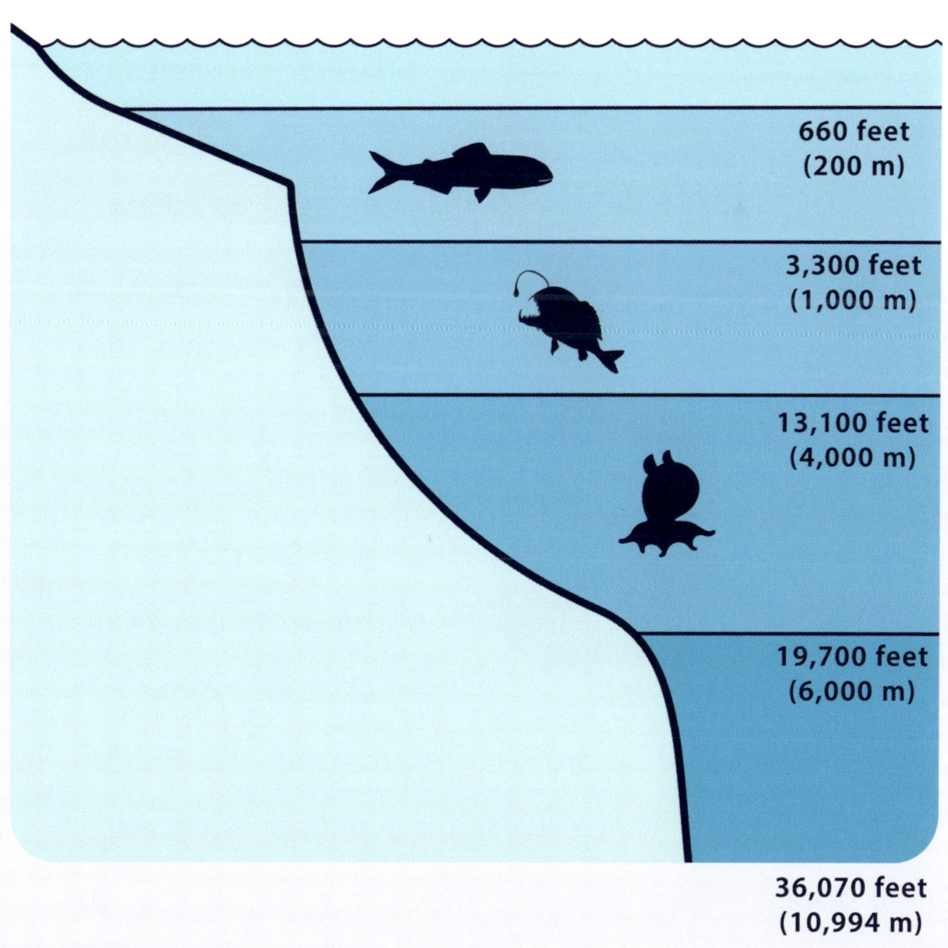

way of luring prey. Instead of searching for food in the dark, anglerfish let food come to them.

Many deep-sea anglerfish species have rods that stick out of their heads. These rods look a bit like fishing poles. At the end of the rods are small sacs of bioluminescent bacteria. These sacs glow in the darkness of the deep sea. The light attracts other fish, which anglerfish then prey on. The mouths of anglerfish are so big that they can swallow fish whole. Because their bodies are very flexible, they can even swallow

THE BLOBFISH

One reason few animals can survive at the bottom of the ocean is the intense water pressure. The weight of the water above is so great that most living things would be crushed beneath it. The blobfish's body is suited to withstand the water pressure. It doesn't have thick bones or muscle. Its body mostly consists of water and fat. When brought up to the water's surface, this fish takes on a very different appearance. Without the water pressure to hold its shape together, it looks like a squishy blob. This is how the fish got its name.

fish that are twice their size. This ability to take in large amounts of food at once helps keep anglerfish alive, even when food is scarce.

The deep sea is home to some very weird animals. But this habitat is not the only one populated by strange creatures. Life on Earth has had a long time to evolve, and this process has produced many weird animals around the world.

EXPLORE ONLINE

Chapter Five discusses deep-sea creatures that stand out from the other creatures in the water. The website below explores deep-sea life. As you know, every source is different. How is the information from the website the same as the information in Chapter Two? What new information did you learn from the website?

DEEP-SEA LIFE

abdocorelibrary.com/weird-animals

FAST FACTS

- The hairy frog grows thick bristles on its sides during mating season. The blood vessels in these bristles help the frog breathe, especially when underwater.
- Natural selection is a process of evolution. It describes how living things change over time.
- Unlike most mammals, the platypus lays eggs. This animal lives in bodies of water in Australia.
- The naked mole rat lives underground in groups. It does not keep a steady internal body temperature.
- The magnificent frigate bird has a relatively large wingspan that allows it to fly for long periods of time. It hunts other birds and forces them to vomit their food, which it then eats.
- Male bowerbirds build elaborate structures called bowers to attract female mates.
- The green basilisk can run on water for short distances.

- Flying snakes flatten their bodies as they fall to glide through the air.
- More than 1,500 different kinds of sea slugs live on Earth. They come in a variety of colors and forms.
- Anglerfish use a bright bulb hanging from their heads to lure prey in the deep ocean.

STOP AND THINK

Tell the Tale

Chapter One of this book discusses hunting hairy frogs in Cameroon. Imagine you are on a similar hunt. Write 200 words about what you see.

Dig Deeper

After reading this book, what questions do you still have about animal adaptations? With an adult's help, find a few reliable sources that can help you answer your questions. Write a paragraph about what you learned.

Say What?

Studying animals can mean learning a lot of new vocabulary. Find five words in this book you've never heard before. Use a dictionary to find out what they mean. Then write the meanings in your own words and use each word in a new sentence.

You Are There

This book discusses several animals found only in Australia. Imagine you are exploring their habitat. Write a letter home telling your friends what you have found. What do you notice about the site? Be sure to add plenty of detail to your notes.

GLOSSARY

architecture
the art of designing and building structures

bioluminescence
the release of light by living things

evolution
the process by which living things change over time

marine
relating to the sea

migrate
to move regularly from one place to another

mollusk
an animal group that includes snails, slugs, mussels, and octopuses

mutation
a change in a living thing's DNA

photosynthesis
the process by which some living things convert sunlight into energy

quadruped
an animal that has four feet

regenerate
to grow back

vertebrate
an animal with a backbone

ONLINE RESOURCES

To learn more about weird animals, visit our free resource websites below.

Visit **abdocorelibrary.com** or scan this QR code for free Common Core resources for teachers and students, including vetted activities, multimedia, and booklinks, for deeper subject comprehension.

Visit **abdobooklinks.com** or scan this QR code for free additional online weblinks for further learning. These links are routinely monitored and updated to provide the most current information available.

LEARN MORE

MacCarald, Clara. *The Weirdest Animals in the World.* BrightPoint, 2024.

Perdew, Laura. *Mammals.* Abdo, 2021.

INDEX

About the Author

Emma Kaiser is a writer and educator based in western Minnesota. She has a master of fine arts in creative writing from the University of Minnesota, and her writing has appeared in many magazines and publications. She is the author of a number of other nonfiction books for students.